DOCTOR JAZZ

# HAYDEN CARRUTH

# Doctor Jazz

COPPER CANYON PRESS

Printed in the United States of America.

Cover art: *The Art of Cool* by Michael Howard.
Copyright 2001 J. Michael Howard Studios.
All rights reserved.

Copper Canyon Press is in residence
under the auspices of the Centrum Founda-
tion at Fort Worden State Park in Port
Townsend, Washington. Centrum sponsors
artist residencies, education workshops for
Washington State students and teachers,
Blues, Jazz, and Fiddle Tunes festivals,
classical music performances, and
the Port Townsend Writers' Conference.

LIBRARY OF CONGRESS
CATALOGING-IN-PUBLICATION DATA

Carruth, Hayden, 1921–
Doctor Jazz: poems / Hayden Carruth.
p. cm.
ISBN 1-55659-163-2 (alk. paper)
ISBN 1-55659-193-4 (paperback edition)
I. Title: Dr. Jazz. II. Title.
PS3505.A77594 D64 2001
811'.54– DC21
2001003556

3 5 7 9 8 6 4 2
FIRST PRINTING
SECOND EDITION

COPPER CANYON PRESS
Post Office Box 271
Port Townsend, Washington 98368
www.coppercanyonpress.org

*Hello Central, give me Doctor Jazz,*
*He's got just what I need, I'll say he has....*

**FERDINAND JELLY ROLL MORTON**

ACKNOWLEDGMENTS

I am grateful to the publishers and editors
of the following periodicals, in which some of
the poems in this book first appeared:
*AGNI, The American Poetry Review,
The American Scholar, Brilliant Corners,
The Café Review, ELF, The Hudson Review,
The Maine Times, Poetry, Poetry International,
Potlatch, The Sewanee Review, Shenandoah,
Sonora Review, Verse,* and *Witness.*

In addition some poems have previously
appeared in two chapbooks: *Three New
Poems,* published by Bradypress of Omaha;
and *Faxes to William,* published by
the Limberlost Press of Boise.

Finally I am especially grateful to the Lannan
Foundation of Santa Fe for support during
the time when the manuscript of this
book was in preparation.

TO

*Gray & Sam*
*Adrienne & Michelle*
*Lois & David*
*Janet & Geof*
*Isabel & Stephen*
*And Joe-Anne*

# CONTENTS

## PART I

# First Scrapbook

*ix*

## PART II

# Martha

## PART III

# The Afterlife

# PART IV

# Faxes

# PART V

# Bashō

# PART VI

# Second Scrapbook

# DOCTOR JAZZ

# PART I

# First Scrapbook

# THE HALF-ACRE OF MILLET

So green the leaves in late September sun
So glossy those dark spikes of seed
Lying between the potatoes and the orchard
A hunting ground for the good king snake
     that searched for shrews
"A tonic for the cows before they go into the barn
     for the long winter,"
Marshall said, and he would turn them into it
How they romped and sang
How they gorged on the sweetness
At last it was trampled and rubbled, the leaves, panicles,
     and stalks were all eaten
And then a day or two later the cows went reluctantly
     to their stanchions
Into the dark muttering and complaining

Now I'm sickly and old and altogether somewhere else
Marshall is a voice from the dusty closet of history
I keep looking for my own half-acre of millet
     in the autumn sun
     but I don't find it
Now I'm told they don't plant millet around here.

# IN PHARAOH'S TOMB

In Pharaoh's tomb the darkness reigns.
    The air was stale and musty.
A thief broke in and stole his eyes
    and wasn't even stealthy.

Pharaoh saw less than he had seen
    before, which seems unlikely.
"Ah, what have I ever done to thee
    that thou so indiscreetly

should'st rob my face?" great Pharaoh cried.
    But the robber was undaunted.
"Shut up, old man. Go back to sleep.
    Vision's not what you wanted."

## OLD SONG FOR THE BO

Hip hop to the auto shop
gonna get us a Jeep with a fringe on top
with bulletproof glass and silver wheels
gonna be the king of the automobiles.

Did anyone ever believe that the dead woman
they buried with a bone needle in her hand
would use it to sew a new jerkin in the country
beyond the moon? Or that the young man whose
mutilated corpse they placed on a shield would
use it to defend himself? No, our ancestors
were not so simple. They did these things
without expectation. They did them in despair.

# BECAUSE I AM

*in mem. Sidney Bechet, 1897–1959*

Because I am a memorious old man
I've been asked to write about you, Papa Sidney,
Improvising in standard meter on a well-known
Motif, as you did all those nights in Paris
And the world. I remember once in Chicago
On the Near North where you were playing with
A white band, how you became disgusted
And got up and sat in front next to the bandstand
And ordered four ponies of brandy; and then
You drank them one by one, and threw the empty
Glasses at the trumpet-player. Everyone laughed,
Of course, but you were dead serious – sitting there
With your fuzzy white head, in your rumpled navy
Serge. When you lifted that brass soprano to your
Lips and blew, you were superb, the best of all,
The first and best, an *Iliad* to my ears.
And always your proper creole name was mis-
Pronounced. Now you are lost in the bad shadows
Of time past; you are a dark man in the darkness,
Who knew us all in music. Out of the future
I hear ten thousand saxophones mumbling
In your riffs and textures, Papa Sidney. And when
I stand up trembling in darkness to recite
I see sparkling glass ponies come sailing at me
Out of the reaches of the impermeable night.

# AGENDA AT 74

Tap barometer, burn trash,
put out seed for birds, tap
barometer, go to market
for doughnuts and Dutch
Masters, feed cat, write
President, tap barometer,
take baby aspirin, write
congressmen, nap, watch
Bills vs. Patriots, tap
barometer, go to post
office and ask Diane if
it's cold enough for her,
go to diner and say "hi,
babe" to Mazie, go to
barbershop and read
*Sports Illustrated,* go
home, take a load off,
tap barometer, go to
liquor store for jug
(Gallo plonk), go
home, pee, etc., sweep
cellar stairs (be careful!),
write letter to editor,
count dimes, count quarters,
tap the fucking barometer...

# OLD MAN'S SLEEP

*for James Laughlin*

Wherever he is, even on Cape Cod
where the gulls slide through the rain
in the tops of the glistening cedars,
where seven young people inhabit
the house, he falls asleep. On the sofa,
reading the poems of his old friend
about Deauville and Munich and Sara-
sota, the life he so envies, and the book
slips from his fingers, he slumps
sideways dreaming of Margaret Shean,
the redhead with whom he went
walking in the woods by Sullivans
Pond in 1934, until his youngest
grandson, amazed in the afternoon,
yells in his face: "Grandpa, Grandpa,
are you sleeping!" Not anymore.
And he awakens, stupid
and confused and ashamed.
"Grandpa, you're weird," the boy says.

# SHOOTING RATS

The war documentary showed
Two GIs on a kind of balcony,
One with a pair of big binoculars,
The other with a high-powered
Rifle and a scope. They had their
Feet propped up on the railing,
They were drinking beer from cans
And smoking cigarettes. The one
With the glasses searched. The one
With the rifle aimed and fired.
The jungle echoed briefly, quietly.
"Got him!" – and they laughed.
It was like a Sunday afternoon
In Vermont when country boys
Shot the rats at the town dump.
I've always felt sorry for the rats.

# TARTAR

They call me Timur the Lame because I caught
a lance-tip in my thigh when I was fifteen
in my first battle, and I've been gimpy ever
since. I lived in Semuscant most of the time,
or in the western parts of my domain, extending
far into the sunset. I could have lived
in Jerusalem, that sty, if I'd wanted. Gimpy
or no, I could ride a horse as well as any
of my people; I believed I was half a horse.
Over the plains like the freaking wind. I killed
300,000 people in my time, and probably
more – Hindus, Persians, Armenians, Jews,
who knows whom? I could speak nine languages
badly. Hard languages. Now like most of the rest
of the world I speak English, an easy language.
English is the language of hell, where I am now
in this grand community, among my friends,
Grant, Napoleon, N'Kruma, Alcibiades, Harry
Truman, Charlemagne, all the great generals.
We speak English and drink bourbon. Some killed
more than I did, some less, but we all did our best.
What's better than the desert reeking with blood?
Generals or conscripts, rich and poor, we know

who we are, everyone, and the gate is open.
Welcome. We're waiting for you, pretty lady.
What do you think hell is if it isn't history?

## AT SEVENTY-FIVE: REREADING AN OLD BOOK

My prayers have been answered, if they were prayers. I live.
I'm alive, and even in rather good health, I believe.
If I'd quit smoking I might live to be a hundred.
Truly this is astonishing, after the poverty and pain,
The suffering. Who would have thought that petty
Endurance could achieve so much?
                                    And prayers –
Were they prayers? Always I was adamant
In my irreligion, and had good reason to be.
Yet prayer is not, I see in old age now,
A matter of doctrine or discipline, but rather
A movement of the natural human mind
Bereft of its place among the animals, the other
Animals. I prayed. Then on paper I wrote
Some of the words I said, which are these poems.

## COFFEE

Coffee. I expect it's a habit you never
fell into. But you're an athlete, I'm
a worker. I drink six or seven cups a day,
and frequently find myself going
to the coffeepot when I need something
to perk me up. The doctor on the radio
said that people over seventy are like
babies, they need lots of sleep and they
need it whenever they want it. Hence
except when I'm really wired on caffeine
I feel as if I'm always drifting off, my head
falling to one side, my vision blurring.
But babies have nothing else to do and
workers always have something to do,
pension or no. Is this merely another
case of the infuriating slipshod nature
of nature? You take your nap without regret,
having done your work-out on schedule.
I drink more and more coffee. Soon both
our hearts will fail, one way or another.

## COLD COFFEE

Cold coffee. In the wintertime he would've
Grimaced and spat it out. Yet now in June,
The middle of the month with a dark sky
Lowering around his house, with flicks of lightning
Nicking the horizon across the wide valley, he
Picks up his half-forgotten cup and the dregs
Are cool and savory. He smiles. The first raindrops
Go plop, plop on the roof of his room. He closes
His eyes. The naked goddess whose perfume
So teases him is plucking the harp she clasps
Between her knees. And the thunder rolls.

# COMPLEYNTE

Somebody knows the way to Tipperary
        But it ain't me.
Somebody is singing "Happy Days" and
        "The Brave and the Free."

All I can see is the eagle dropping his
        Mess on the ground,
And every day I go to look for my mind
        At the Lost & Found.

Whatever happened to the Sewanee River
        Way down souf?
How come I wasn't born with a nickelodeon
        In my mouf?

# ECONOMICS

*for Robin Ward*

Well, Mr. C, he's somewhat weird.
Worms are living in his beard.
He gives them to the fisher trade
Who bring him trout and pike and bass
With which his hunger is allayed
While he sits comfy on his ass.

# HOME POME

From B. Goodman's "Flying Home" to P. Goodman's
"The Lordly Hudson," ain't it a hell of a good feeling
To be here again? Brother, there I was
In Totowa, New Jersey, a town I found I couldn't
Even pronounce, driving helter-skelter for an hour
Among shopping plazas, used-car dealers, pizza joints,
Motels, hotels, and regular whorehouses, I couldn't
Have been more alien if I'd come from Mars – looking
For a friendly face. I couldn't even find a willow tree.
Two days. Then I drove my junker onto 80 West.
West! Heading into the winter sky, into the Poconos,
To Clarks Summit, Binghamton, and then up 26
Through the Chenango country, and here I am,
My dears. You welcome me one and all, my
Beautiful ardent woman, my handsome son,
My dog, my two cats, and my sympathetic woodstove.

# NANA

Nana was a Gibson girl, with gleaming auburn hair
that fell to her waist when she let it. Every morning
a hundred strokes on the right side, a hundred more
on the left, then the same again at night, and when
she piled it up on top in swirls and twists and spirals
and set a monumental hat on top of that
she could walk down Broadway as gracefully as a
full-rigged schooner parting the waves. Nana
had no money, but the guys she hung out with
had plenty, and that made all the difference. She dined
at Delmonico's and Luchow's, danced at the Waldorf,
went to the opera twice a week at least, and to the
billiard tournaments in Madison Square every month.
To the end she retained a canny trace of the British
accent she was born with. Her dresses showed
an ample and enticing bosom, I'm sure, with necklaces
from Cartier to set it off. When her daughter –
that's Margery, my mother – came, Nana grew tired
of marriage and divorced her husband, a scandal in
the 1890s, but then she grew tired of scandal
and married again, a man so obnoxious to his
stepdaughter that Margery ran away at sixteen
and never returned. What became of my step-
grandfather? I have no idea, but he was shucked

one way or another. And Nana lived alone.
Once a year she traveled by train up into the
awful countryside to visit her grandson and bring him
presents from Wanamaker's, huge boxes wrapped
in tinsel. In her fifties she became enthusiastically
converted to Christian Science, but then disease
attacked – cancer probably, though I don't know.
Imagine her misery, uncured yet hopeful, alone
in her hotel on upper Broadway. She grew tired.
She flumped, as we newspaper people used to say,
from the fifteenth floor, and that was the end of Nana.
That was the end of presents from Wanamaker's.
That was the end of watching, once a year, while she
brushed her long gleaming tresses with her hairbrush
that had a naked woman in silver on the back.
How strange to be thinking of her now, a century
gone by, worlds and worlds away, she whom I
scarcely knew, a spark in my difficult mind.
Nana was a Gibson girl, with gleaming auburn hair.
She went down with her hair flying behind like flame
in the scintillating darkness of the Manhattan night.

# NEW PARAGRAPH

One hoped the brilliant sunset of July
In all its layered upsurge, orange and rose,
Might fade more slowly from the sky
And bring the day to close
On something more concordant than this cry
In massive, horrifying dark. To nullify
Is what the once appealing night
Means now, to rend, to disunite.
Down-pressing dark! Obliteration spills
Like ink upon a page
Enshrouding words in blackness. Oblivion shrills
Like all of noise, of meaning, rage
Enraged, terror self-terrorized. Ascend
No more, and never more effect, engage
Not ever. This is the unending end.

## OLD MAN SUCCUMBING TO RETROSPECTION

How his mind was always filled with music    How
he strove and strove from the age of fifteen
in an orchard clouded with applebloom to the age
of seventy-five in this so small and shabby room
strove to invent a poem that would cry out
in the variable textures of Bechet's soprano sax
or Webster's tenor soaring growling whispering
How he always failed    How he toiled
as the years came more and more to press
upon his will although he nevertheless never
permitted himself to give up    How he says
to himself now Is this a life    And how it must be
for what else can it be    How he would have liked
even so something more    Or something a little less.

# POLITICAL CONSIDERATIONS

What it means is not beclouded, but Joe-Anne says
       they take after me and who am I
to say otherwise? These plants, I mean, which I
       grow outdoors and in to gratify

my instinct for what goes on in the dirt, all
       that rucklemuck and feverishness:
my plants are base, spoiled, aggressive, and self-willed.
       Like me. That's a fact. My hibiscus,

for instance, that she gave me when she first moved in,
       a seedling in a plastic pot, and now
about to grow through the roof – it will if
       I don't top it soon. It's got one bough

that would make a bed for Odysseus home
       from his wanderings, and that's the truth,
right there in my living room. And then out next
       to the old stone wall in its uncouth

dishevelment, my roses and daylilies –
       an NFL game that never ends,
the Southside Roses vs. the Orange Dragons
       all afternoon. While the Dragons send

their fastest runners downfield, the Roses bash
        bud-heads in the line. Bands play, mascots
tumble, fans go wild, and the players bloom like
        fury, clashing – it's like apricots

and strawberries all smashed together. Meanwhile
        the sycamore shouts, the box elder
sprouts new arms, the peonies gape and bellow,
        the grapes run onto the field, the fir

dances, and it's a mêlée, believe me. Joe-
        Anne says my green thumb is bloody. She's
convinced I have to quit for my sake, and hers,
        and everyone's, i.e., for world peace.

# STABAT MATER

Standing, her eyes cast down. Standing
Before the sea-wave black with oil,
The liquefying gulls in travail at her feet,
Their sunken departing eyes, and before
The grassless prairie scorched and raveling
Like an old Indian blanket, the forest
Smirched, the river gorged with rust
Winding through valleys which once shone
Green, and before the child whose pain
Is so great no tears will come to its crusted
Face, the mother who bore us, who held us,
Who delighted all our hours, standing
With downcast eyes... Standing.

# STINK

Sweat. For that I have perspired like a pig in Miami
     all my days.
Tobacco. For that I have consumed bales of burley
     and I eat cigars for breakfast.
Semen. For that from my great flume have poured
     repeated sluices always.
Alcohol. For that my bones have been soaked in a
     firth of whiskey.
Grease. What did you expect from an old
     grease monkey?
Methane. For that I am a bean-eater and a consumer
     of succulent meats.
Feet. For that I have a black toe where someone dropped
     a piano on it when I wasn't looking.
Must. For that it has been seeping from me on every one
     of my 27,375 days.
Ashes. Well, can you possibly think I'm not a starving poet
     in a garret?

# STONES AGAIN

When I was a young man I carried pebbles not in my mouth
        – that idiocy! – but in my pocket, smooth pebbles
of different colors, and when I found a larger stone I liked
        I took it home, including slates from the Keene Valley
and pyrites from Arizona. Once I wrote a book about
        a man obsessed with a stone, a whole book. Now I'm old.
I pick up these stones and drop them into the wagon and haul
        them with my little John Deere up the hill – putt,
            putt, putt –
to the thornapple thicket. Some of the stones are heavy, some
        have edges that break the frail skin of my hands. Anyway
I'm too short-winded for this work. My cigar has gotten too
        short too, it singes my beard, and burnt hair is the most
awful smell in all the world. So what do I feel about stones
        now? No doubt I'm an idiot after all because
what comes to mind is a question. If like Deucalion I throw
        these stones behind me will they turn into
           grandchildren?

# THE HERON

Let me tell you, my dear, about the heron I saw
by the edge of Dave Haflett's lovely little pond.
A great blue heron, standing perfectly still, where it
had been
studying Dave's rainbows and brookies beneath the surface.
And I too stood perfectly still – as perfectly as I could –
not twenty feet away, each of us contemplative and quiet.
Communication occurred. I felt it. Not just simple
wonder and apprehension, but curiosity and concern.
It was evident. The great bird in its heraldic presence,
so beautifully marked, so poised against the dark green water.
I in my raggedness, with my cigarette smoldering,
my eyes
squinting, my cap tilted back. Two invisibly beating hearts.
Then the impetus lapsed. The heron nodded and
flew away.
I turned back into Dave's workshop and picked up a wrench.
If goodness exists in the world – and it does – then
this moment
was the paradigm of it, a recognition, a life in conjunction with
a life.
But why am I compelled to tell you about it? It was
wordless.
And why, over and over again, must I write this poem?

# THE SOUND

When I was a boy at this time of year
I lay on the near side of our small meadow
in the tall grass and listened to the bees
on the far side in the honey locust
trees. I couldn't see them, or the trees
either, hidden as I was in the grass,
but the sound was loud and somehow
sweet – the humming of innumerable
bees, as Tennyson would have said.
The sound seemed everywhere as I
gazed at the sky, enclosed in my sweet
grave in the grass. *This is how the sound
of the invisible stars singing would be,*
I said, *if only I could hear them.*

# PART II
# Martha

# DEAREST M—

### THE FIRST DAY OF HER DEATH
### (AS RECORDED BY HER FATHER)

In November when the days are short and dim
        she died. In November
when the Baldwin apple tree retains
hundreds of its bright apples, each bejeweled
        with a sparkle of snow
        under our gray Oneidan sky,
she died. She was Martha. She was my daughter.

A strange, unnatural thing is it – to outlive
        one's daughter.
I go repeatedly, repeatedly, to stand and gaze
        out my window
as if with my glaring eye I could blast
the ornamented Baldwin into nonexistence
        and bring down all,
as if the tree were good and evil, as if
        the world meant something.
Yes, the waves and buffets of all humanity's
desperation shake me like a leaf,
        although I stand stock-still.

The immensity of what should be said
            defeats me. Language
like a dismasted hulk at sea is overwhelmed
            and founders.

            Only last week Sappho
lay in the arms of some sleek adolescent
on her green and golden isle
and coughed – barked like a seal –
            and died.

And then a lifetime ago the pediatrician
examined her, eyes, ears, mouth,
heart and lungs, hands and feet, and finally
with expert thumbs he parted her tiny vulva
three days old, looked and stood back.
            "Perfect," he said. "She's perfect." Was this
the first of all of her triumphant indignities?

            In a cold puff of air, as if
thousands of invisible and soundless feet
            were marching by,
the apple tree sways briefly and stands still.

Looking "nearly weightless" (I was told) she lay
like a young crone,
            who had been as beautiful and sexy
as any young woman you could care to meet;

riddled with cancer, wracked by pneumonia,
comatose in a stupor of morphine, attached
by tubes and wires to the gleaming apparatus.
        And slowly
the intelligence receded from her eyes.

        Slowly the shadow fades
        from a footprint in the snow.

"Don't hurt the snow, don't hurt the snow!" she cried
as I pulled on my gloves and lifted
the shovel to my shoulder by the door,
she who became a painter and who now is
        the painter forever,
all these images of earthly splendor and fascination
        on our walls,
from here to California.

Three deer have come to the apple tree, pawing the snow
for fallen, frozen apples. One of them, a young doe,
rises on her bent back legs with her forelegs
hanging and helpless, to reach an apple on the tree,
        but she cannot –
this defeated, humble, supplicative gesture.
Yet even pathos remains futile. Can anything arouse
passion in an old man like the death of a young
woman? The desire to smash something,
        but what's the good

of littering the floor with splintered glass?
Nothing is worth smashing. And then,
out of character, beyond reason, it is
        sexual too.
The evil desire to fuck someone so that she'll
stay fucked once and for all. It's true, one thinks,
        God must be a female.
Who else would so humiliate a hungry doe?


Martha did her painting in private. We rarely
        saw her at work.
If by chance we did, she would stand pointedly
in front of her easel, shielding the canvas
from our view. Similarly, she did not talk
about her painting, perhaps because she was
self-taught and didn't know the words –
        but that's nonsense.
She was as language-driven as her father,
she had plenty of words. But process was
something she did not wish to discuss.
        Her paintings
were neither representational nor abstract.
She painted what she saw, supplying color and contrast
from the deepest recesses of her imagination,
        as when one dreams
of what one has seen just before falling asleep.
        An outdoor table and umbrella
by the sea with a white sailboat in the distance

and the shadow of the umbrella falling just so,
steeply pitched, across the astonishing pineapple
        and the bottle of wine.
Can a father recover his daughter in a painting?
Or in an orange-and-umber blouse he gave her
        ten years ago?
Well, sometimes the heart in its excess enacts
such pageantry. But it is hollow, hollow.

She died, as she had lived for many years,
        far away.
No doubt my life is more deficient
because I didn't see her expiration. Yet
she could not have known, could not
have twitched her eyelid if I had kissed her
then. The last she said to me, on the phone
        five days before,
was, "Don't grieve for me. That would spoil everything."
As if amidst such spoilage one more tiny ounce
        could make a difference.
Clearly her view of what was happening was
not like mine. My dear, I hope I may
somehow when my turn – soon now – comes
attain your view. But I'm not confident.
An old man is such a frail effigy
in the garden of beautiful young women.

Palinuro was a young man. He was dark
and strong, good-looking, an Assyrian perhaps
        or an African,
a songwriter in his spare time, my friend,
who had been recruited to be the helmsman
on the voyage to Italy, our voyage of conquest.
When the great storm struck, a mountain
of water rose up high beside the ship, towering
in its immensity, shutting out the sky,
and fell across the decks, sweeping Palinuro
overboard. In an instant, an instant, Palinuro
        vanished beneath the waves.

We know his name, yet even that was
probably invented by some poet. What we
        truly know
are death and taxes. These are indubitable.
Martha also had her share of problems in the tax
department. She was a worrier. She schemed
and figured endlessly to pay the vigorish,
which is what she called the health insurance
premiums. Usury on a borrowed life.
Her worries were at least a little distraction
        from her pain.

I'll write a check, a paltry amount but all I
can afford, and send it to my grandchildren.

Martha was married twice, and no man could ask
for better sons to be brought to him by a daughter.
Ames, the musician and entomologist. Then Jerome,
so fittingly named, who cared for her in her illness
selflessly, with abiding affection. Abiding.
Affection was his abode. He is a saint, and who
can imagine now how achingly he is bereft.
Ames too, wherever he is – I think somewhere
in Virginia. This is what we know. This
is everything we know, all that we can share
ultimately. Loss. Loneliness. How appropriate
that knowledge in the bible meant having
sexual intimacy with. The impossible incest.
The illusion of connectedness. Loss in having.

And have we this time reached the culmination?
Martha died in what is called the Age of
Terror – carnage at the airport, bleeding
bodies strewn everywhere, even in the great temple
          at Luxor. This also
is what we know, the continual orgy. The rictus
of death and orgasm. We know that Mother Cosmos
is the greatest terrorist, mailing out letter bombs
every day from her empyrean agency to addresses
          all over the world.

When she was thirteen she had a bathing cap
that made her look, she thought, like a movie star –

a cap made of rubber, close-fitting, white and ribbed. She
wore it all summer. Why not? Even while she was reading
　　*Catcher in the Rye.*

The light is changing. Twilight has come, a peculiar
light, pellucid on the snow even in our
gloomy climate. The apple tree appears to step forward
as if out of Stygian semidarkness, for my greater
approval – the beautiful apple tree. Martha
did not live in a gloomy climate but in the sun,
in a southern place, and when she lay
in her bikini beside the swimming pool
it was as if Phidias himself had placed her there.

A few years later, how scarred she was! The surgeons
left their welts all over her, front and back.
At one time for a year or two they even
planted a pump in her abdomen. Yes, a pump!
A gadget of plastic parts that would direct
chemicals to her liver. She carried it
like a horrible fetus long past the normal
term, but it would not be born. And yet
it moved in her and spoke to her – a whisper –
the child she loathed and feared. Has it been
born now, a dreadful cesarean? My newest
grandchild – a pump? No doubt that's one way
　　　　to look at it.

The first day of Martha's death is over. What
        of the night?

The apple tree is gone. Eurydice has gone back
to hell, weeping and grim, betrayed. The night
is Pluto's cave. I've turned on all the lights
in this little house on the hill, my defiance
of metaphysical reality and the Niagara-Mohawk
Power Corporation. Idly, as so often, I am
staring at my watch, the numbers clicking away,
hours, minutes, seconds, but time is the most
unrealizable quantity. How long has Eurydice
been gone – a moment or always? And now
suddenly the lights go off. Something somewhere
is broken. The autumn wind has blown down
a tree across the lines. Where did I put that candle
I used to have? Somewhere a glitch is glitching, yet
this is a familiar place, I can move in the dark.
Martha was dead for two minutes, then two hours,
then ten, and will it become a day, two days, with her
not here? Impossible. I cannot think of it.
Yet the lighted numbers on my watch keep turning,
ticking and turning. The numbered pages of my books
smolder on my shelves, surrounding me. Alas, my dear,
alas. Time and number are a metaphysical reality
        after all.

Motherhood came to Martha when she was sixteen.
She "fruited early," as I said at the time in a
poem. She came to live with me, a Southern belle
among backwoods Yankees, and she carried it off
beautifully. Enrolled in the local high school,
took her lessons home when they told her
she had become too big and was an embarrassment,
graduated handily, whereupon Ames
graduated from his school too and came north,
and they were married in our house, a moving
little ceremony witnessed by a couple of
neighboring farmers. They went to live in a trailer
on the north side of the settlement. Martha
scarcely made it to the hospital when her time came,
and half an hour later it was all over
and I was a grandfather at the age of forty-eight –
which was not unusual in that region.
The two young people were good parents. This
was the era of the Stones, Joan Baez singing
"We Shall Overcome," the trial of the Chicago
Seven. Martha asked us to baby-sit sometimes
when her class schedule demanded it, and also
occasionally in the evenings when she and Ames
wanted to go out to smoke a little grass and get
mildly tanked. Why not? They and their friends
were in and out of our house continually,
and it was a happy time. But eventually
they moved away to the west to continue their

educations, and our enforced separation – Martha's
and mine – resumed. What is a father who has been
lost in the wreckage of divorce? The first time
Martha saw me (i.e., when she was able to see,
being four years old), she clung to her mother's skirt
and pointed at me and twisted her little body
in a kind of agony and said, "Mama, who is that
young man?" She had been "prepared" for the meeting,
obviously. But what preparation was possible, then
          or ever?

Soon we shall come to the festival of lights that the
          little girl so loved. It must have been
a wonderful festival before the Cathocapitalist Church
destroyed it. He can just dimly remember lighted
          candles on a tree.

Faces fade in and out of his dreams like the lights
across the valley through the shifting bare branches
          of November.

5:00 AM. Peering out into the windy dark.
A confused and windy head, aged and trembling.
Yet the coffee tastes as astounding as ever, delicious
in the morning darkness, the fragrant tobacco smoke
is soothing. I haven't shed a tear. What an awful
heritage this great goddamned American, prairie-Baptist
stoicism is! I blame it on my grandmother's influence –

Ettie from Minnesota, in the eighties of the last
century. But it is everywhere. I would wail and keen,
I would shriek, I would writhe like a Hindu in the street!
        Believe me, it would be a pleasure.

In darkness the numbers on my watch twitch
        in their permutations.
5:14, 5:15 – I stare at them. Something mysterious
about these instantly altering forms, something
        mordant and implacable.
Usually I take off my watch at night
        before I sleep, but last night I forgot.

In early, windy light the apple tree
dances wildly, flinging her apples as if
        they were a shawl –
strange apparition of flamenco in
        snowy upstate New York.

Instead, this gush of words, this surging elegy.
From a poet who has been blocked and almost silent
for two years. Yes, the human emotional
mechanism in all its gut-eating horridness
cannot be denied. A release of some dire kind
has been accomplished. How shaming, how
offensive! And like all elegiac words, these swirl
around the question forever unanswered: "What for? What
        is it all for?"

Born in Chicago, 6 December 1951. Parents divorced when she was an infant. Lived in Auburn, Alabama, with maternal grandparents, then with mother and stepfather. Public school. Married first, Ames Herbert; one son, Britton. Married second, Jerome Ward; two sons, Hayden and Robin. AB, Northern Arizona Univ., Flagstaff; MA, Arizona State Univ., Tempe. Cancer diagnosis, California, 1990. Died, Birmingham, 17 November 1997.

When I remarried – "What?" she laughed. "Again?" –
she took to her new stepmother quickly.
They were the same age. They conducted long
conversations by phone, laughing and teasing,
sweet to my overhearing ears. We were a family
after all. We visited back and forth, as families do,
and spent a vacation together on Cape Cod.
That is, until I became too old and ill to travel.

Sunrise at last, if you can call it that.
      Above the horizon
at the top of the steep eastern hill,
a faint disk has appeared, a dim useless moon
      behind the overcast.

First thing every morning, before I did anything else,
        I used to write to her.
Coffee and cigarettes. I'd sit in the kitchen
in my Morris chair, unsling my laptop, and type
        "Dearest M" –
then I'd spin out anything I could think of that might
distract her for a moment from her pain.
Nonsense, trivia, I used to complain that, alas,
        I am not Marcus Aurelius.
Wisdom for a dying daughter? I had none.
But at least I knew whom I was addressing.
For an hour every morning we were in touch.
I in my old bathrobe, she in her tousled bed,
her brown curls shadowing her smile. For years
she smiled, often she laughed, and the pain-marks
on her lovely face would disappear. When she was told,
back at the beginning, that she had no more than six
months to live, she learned how to live with death
        almost immediately.

Whom am I addressing now? Not Martha. The absence
        is like a hollow in my mind.
Christ, is there no mercy! But of course the concept
        is unnatural.
Her friends then? But I think they care little
        for poetry.
Twenty years ago I'd have made a box,
I'd have planed and sanded, glued the dovetails

neatly, driven the little brass screws of the hinges
with a watchmaker's screwdriver, and chiseled
a sunflower and her initials into the lid. I used to love
        to make boxes.

The telephone is ringing. Somebody wants
to sell him a piece of land in Arizona. He thinks
briefly of the high country around Payson
that he has admired so much, the great forest
of pines. The phone rings again. Already
Martha has been cremated. Already people
are busy making arrangements, establishing
times and places. But he knows he will not
go to the funeral. He could not bear to hear
that mumbo-jumbo intoned over the cold
        ashes of his daughter.

        As a child she was like
        the sapling birch that grew
        at the end of the orchard,
        slim and graceful, fresh
        in the morning light.
        Then she became
        like Diana running naked
        in the woods, standing
        among the deer and hazel
        trees. On her thirtieth
        birthday she was everyone's

delight, the dream-woman
of men, the athletic
and wise preceptor
of women. And now,
except in a father's memory,
she has dispersed
and gone, so soon,
so soon.

Noon is the ominous hour. Not midnight
when we celebrate our joy. Not dusk or dawn
when we take our pills and sit back to
consider. Noon is the ominous hour.
The puny sun mounts toward the apogee
and a thin curtain of snow begins to fall.
A father's vision becomes fluttery,
like his breath. He has reached the end
of the first day of his daughter's death. His sight
is hazy as he looks out at the apple tree.

# PART III
# The Afterlife

# THE AFTERLIFE:
## REMEMBERING MATCHES

*in mem. J.L.*

Once when I was an old poet and was visiting
An even older poet, he dropped a box
Of matches that scattered every whichway
At our feet, and although he asked me not to,
I stooped to help him retrieve them and restore them
Neatly to their box, the red ends pointing
All in the same direction. What a delight –
One of those little moments of gratification
That Saint Augustine says are the only value
In life and the presages of a divine presence.
My friend was a great man, and so in a far
Less significant way was I, and I helped him
Return his scattered matches to their little box.

## THE AFTERLIFE:
## REMEMBERING FUCKING

When I sank into you I felt warmth
Against warmth, flesh against flesh, vitality
Against vitality, and it was great, my dear,
It was magnificent. And then our passion rose –
Not that it wasn't pretty high already –
And we throbbed together, sweat-slick bellies
Slapping, I held you in a vise-like
Embrace and you dug your nails into
My back and wrapped your legs around me,
And then we came, two together in that
Great enigma, I not knowing what orgasm
Felt like to you and you not knowing what
Orgasm felt like for me – the impenetrable
Mystery. "Everything is possible," Chuang Tzu
Said, "If one only gives oneself to another."

## THE AFTERLIFE:
## TIME AND THE CHERRY TREE

When I looked out in early light
I saw a whiteness there, slight in the little
Sour cherry half across the yard, and I thought,
The snow has come, snow in the night,
Because in late October, now, the first snow
Often arrives, and we'd set back our clocks
Two nights ago.
             But then when the great sun,
Beneficent, arose, I saw in a suffusing illumination
Cherry blossoms, the tree was flowering, actually
Flowering there in my sight, although
The little cherry had died two years ago
And I in sorrow had left it standing dead
Because it was so graceful, so shapely
And delicate, even if the waxwings no longer
Come for its fruit.
             I said, Why shouldn't the dead
Tree bloom, making its soft effulgence spread
In October, now, for my so amended vision? This,
After great change, is what affection does.

## THE AFTERLIFE:
### LETTER TO SAM HAMILL I

You may think it strange, Sam, that I'm writing
a letter in these circumstances. I thought
it strange too – the first time. But there's
a misconception I was laboring under, and you
are too, viz., that the imagination in your
vicinity is free and powerful. After all,
you say, you've been creating yourself all
along imaginatively. You imagine yourself
playing golf or hiking in the Olympics or
writing a poem and then it becomes true.
But you still have to do it, you have to exert
yourself, will, courage, whatever you've got, you're
mired in the unimaginative. Here I imagine a letter
and it's written. Takes about two-fifths of a
second, your time. Hell, this is heaven, man.
I can deluge Congress with letters telling
every one of those mendacious sons of bitches
exactly what he or she is, in maybe about
half an hour. In spite of your Buddhist
proclivities, when you imagine bliss
you still must struggle to get there. By the way
the Buddha has his place across town on
Elysian Drive. We call him Bud. He's lost weight
and got new dentures, and he looks a hell of a

lot better than he used to. He always carries
a jumping jack with him everywhere just
for contemplation, but he doesn't make it
jump. He only looks at it. Meanwhile Sidney
and Dizzy, Uncle Ben and Papa Yancey, are
over by Sylvester's Grot making the sweetest,
cheerfullest blues you ever heard. The air,
so called, is full of it. Poems are fluttering
everywhere like seed from a cottonwood tree.
Sam, the remarkable truth is I can do any
fucking thing I want. Speaking of which
there's this dazzling young Naomi who
wiped out on I-80 just west of Truckee
last winter, and I think this is the moment
for me to go and pay her my respects.
Don't go way. I'll be right back.

## THE AFTERLIFE:
## LETTER TO SAM HAMILL II

For the record, Sam, it's worth pointing out
we are blessed here with a splendid number
of splendid females, going by such names as
Cleo and Antoinette, Godiva and Pocahontas –
in fact we have a song we sing sometimes,
"Poking Pocahontas." *Poking Pocahontas
in her little fauntas is a hell of a good way
to spend a summer's day,* etc. Course it makes
dear old Pokey madder than a wet hen,
and Cap Smith too, but we don't mean harm
and they know it. That's what this place is all
about. In this community harm is something
we're glad to get along without, absolutely
delighted in fact. But I'm losing my way. What
I wanted to say is that I've been out here
ten years now – is that right? (I lose track
of what you call time) – and there's really only
one womanly essence in the place. It's peculiar,
yet she is every one of them. You know her.
Blue almond eyes, auburn locks that flow
across her shoulders, a wide brow and slightly
hollow cheeks, a full beguiling mouth,
a neck like a gazelle's, breasts like the swelling
sonorities of clarinets in one of Beethoven's

early chamber pieces, long arms and legs,
a middle part that sometimes resembles a wheatfield
in a slow breeze and sometimes a vine that twines
in a banyan tree. Her sweet thoughts occur
in my mind continually. That's the way it is.
Her touch is breakfast, lunch, dinner, and supper.
Her desire is the language of every song I sing.
What a subsistence, Sam! You can't conceive it.

## THE AFTERLIFE:
### CATS

They were everywhere, part of the landscape, part
of the cityscape. Now the souls of the cats
are like mosquitoes. Orange tabbies, little black-and-
whites, big gray ones, Manx, coon cats from Maine,
the longhaired white beauties. Domesticated
by the ancient Egyptians and Babylonians, who
called them *mi-mi* and *tzikik,* sacred names,
but they were known on the Mongolian steppes
as well. I remember the purple cat I saw
sitting discontentedly on the abutment
of a bridge in Central Park – someone had
painted him. I remember my own cats, Tanio,
Mr. Tolliver, Nose, and Smudgie, and the rest.
Now the souls of the cats arrive each day
from the crematoria and killing chambers
of the SPCA, great hecatombs of cats. Ah,
it would be dismaying if at this point in my
peculiar existence I were capable of dismay.
But what is, is. Mostly the souls of cats
are assigned to the division of the Working Poor.

## THE AFTERLIFE:
## PSYCHOTROPICS


Well, one has to come to terms, right?
        With the Greeks and Romans,
even the Akkadians, even
        with Newt Gingrich –

that's what we were told. So
        someone invented
the Wonder Drugs. First
        it was Thorazine,

followed by Nardil, Elavil,
        Valium, Pamelor,
Dalmane, and Halcion, Zoloft,
        Xanax, Prozac –

think of the poet who made up
        all those names!
And my brain, which had been
        frazzled from the beginning,

became altogether scrambled.
        Now here I am,
a mere husk if that,
        scrambled forever.

## THE AFTERLIFE:
## LETTER TO STEPHEN DOBYNS I

You live in a sinking nation, Stephen, in a stinking
Time. America is falling apart. We look down in
Astonishment, but mostly in dismay. The other day
When I met Mr. Jefferson and Mr. Madison
On the plaza they turned their backs on me. I
Understood them. I'm a recent arrival, tainted
With degeneracy, no matter what my personal
State of innocence or guilt. Alas, they say
They can tell it in my speech. They say the spectacle
Of presidents and professors impeached on charges
Of trivial misconduct for patently greedy
And partisan ends is more than they can stand.
Who would have thought America could become
A nation where the putsch, the coup, the revolution
Of the swine could prevail against the common
Will. Stephen, we conclude the common will
Isn't strong enough, not anymore, the corruption
Has reached so deep and spread so far. You
Must learn again to live in the common shame,
As in the days of slavery and the massacres of the
Natives. You must learn to live again in
Dreadful isolation, a castaway. Oh, Stephen,
For the first time I'm actually glad I've escaped,
Even to the nullity of the afterlife, even in spite
Of all the beauty and comradeship I've lost.

# THE AFTERLIFE:
## LETTER TO STEPHEN DOBYNS II

The most painful image I have now, here, is
Not the photograph I saw all my earthly life
Of people bombed somewhere, people starving,
Or even the brains of the cyclist dripping, egglike,
From the hood of that Pontiac when I was a child.
Stephen, it's Dizzy blowing his horn. His head,
Distended like a grotesque balloon, cheeks, neck,
His throat, even his temples, bulging like nothing
I ever saw, some monstrous fruit about to burst,
Blood and flesh all over the bandstand. A flap
Of lip-meat draped on top of a music rack,
For instance. Why did he let himself come
To play like that? We don't know; he didn't
Know. But he said it didn't hurt. Yet still
I cringe with the pain of it whenever that face
Comes on the screen. And then the sound track,
That brilliance, that clarity and force, that
Extraordinary originality. It is so beautiful.
I soar, it seems, I actually used to levitate,
Writhing in his tortured love. This,
I think, is why the image stays. I know,
He knew, everyone must know that beauty
Is always, always, accompanied by pain.

# PART IV

# Faxes

# FAXES TO WILLIAM

### ONE

Some poets write blurbs, William,
and some do not. And it is by
a law of nature that the former
envy the latter desperately
though they, the former, can do
nothing to release themselves
from the trap, squirm and prevaricate
as they may. They have unmade
their beds and they must schlepp in them.

### TWO

The news announces that research now shows
aspirin to be a preventative for certain cancers.
Joe-Anne who every morning insists she has a
headache cries out in glee,
"You see!
I've been doing the right thing for years!"

## THREE

The man who has a lifelong intimate relationship
with death, who thinks of death continually,
whose sexual and esthetic behavior is determined
by death, whose ordinary perceptions and routines
of work are shadowed by death, nevertheless
hides his obsession or disguises it in hundreds
of devious and nearly unconscious demeanors,
and then he wonders, he always wonders,
if everyone else is doing the same thing.


FOUR

William, you are a fisherman. It seems
as if all my friends are fishermen.
You know every trout stream and salmon river
in New England, the Maritimes, and Michigan.
You sit in your tiny room with hundreds of
boxes of feathers, wires, fabric, I don't know what,
and tie flies, exquisite flies, works of art,
which you frame behind glass for your friends,
and at night when you dream as like as not
it's of some particular stretch of shining water
you've read about in Scotland or Peru.
William, I hate fishing. I hate to kill.
Killing even a nearly brainless pike or a

totally brainless broccoli unnerves me. I long
to come to nature not as an intruder killing
and ravaging but as a compleat insider, one
of the fraternity, paid up and at my ease
forever. But I hate to kill. William, how
can we be friends? How can I be a poet?

## FIVE

In this transition, William,
     from winter to spring
today in the pasture
     I was up looking

at the runoff, the damage
     of washout and rivulet.
That pasture is about
     as wet as it can get.

It's almost as if the sea
     withdrew from the strand
this morning, leaving me
     this new found land.

Well, you know that
     long low spot

crossways on the downside
      of the ledge outcrop?

It was still full of snow.
      Snow lay in the swale
of my hill pasture
      like Ahab's white whale.


SIX

I came to this nearly anonymous
town, William, four years ago
to make myself completely anonymous,
me with my social security and my
little house on the hill. And now?
These nearly anonymous bastards
have increased my assessment 3.5
times. That's three point five! Taking
advantage of an exiled poet, the shits.
They better watch out, I'll spread their
rotten town all over the map for the rest
of time! Well, for a few years anyway.

## SEVEN

William, when the cat
starts to throw up
– convulsing and gagging –
there's really nothing to do
but sit still and watch it.

## EIGHT

When a bug flies into your mouth,
William, and dies and you
can't get it out so eventually
you swallow it, afterward
for an hour you still feel
a little nasty after-lump
in the middle of your throat.

## NINE

William, where the dancing saffron
butterfly disappeared within
the shadow of the sumac
grove I saw
the apparition of a hideous naked
old man peering out.

### TEN

Every year, William,
I say I'll note
not the first but the last
firefly of the season,
but then they're gone,
vanished undetected.
Tonight is motionless.
Where they go, William,
is what we know, not when.
Does it make any difference?

### ELEVEN

How the hell does a butterfly fly
against the wind? How does she
fly through the rain? Don't give me
your precise scientific answers, William.
They don't mean a thing. Precisely.

### TWELVE

Weddings, William –
what are we
to think of them?

For my part at least
I'd sooner be
married by an apple tree
than by a priest.


<br>

THIRTEEN

The fallen hibiscus flower
that was so exotic, intricate, and splendid
lay on the floor, a reddish
pulpy mess. I took it
to the container of unpleasantness
for the compost heap. Inevitably,
William, hopelessly I thought
of all the poems I've written.


<br>

FOURTEEN

Let me tell you, William,
something crucial, something
absolutely basic, with which
I know you'll agree. Otherwise
we have no basis for this
colloquy. Justice can never
contain injustice. I don't care
what the President says.

### FIFTEEN

William, for the things
life didn't give us
we have no
compensation. None.

### SIXTEEN

Yes. William, I've been,
God knows, a complainer. It was
either that or silence. Poets
are deprived of stoicism.

### SEVENTEEN

Nothing on land, William, nothing
Equals a storm at sea. You watch
100,000 tons of water rise
Mountainously from nowhere,
Warrump, before you, above you,
And you know what a trifling
Nervous squiggle you are in the
Cosmos of elemental energy.
Fortunately this happened to me
Fifty years ago, and since then
I've lived in monotonous delusion.

For some of us, William,
whom you call fools and poets
the death of love is the death of life
however long the blood and breath endure.
And this is knowledge. And knowledge
cannot be dissipated
by a song.

William, do you know why
I like writing these faxes
to you? Because you
don't have a fax machine.

Sometimes, William, a swallow of coffee
goes down your esophagus like an orange
going down an ostrich. It's gross, William,
it's disconcerting. Why must we be reminded
that Nature can be as corrupt as Congress?

### TWENTY-ONE

The wise man's wisdom
is often hidden, William,
because he can't find a way
to break into the conversation.

### TWENTY-TWO

Now, William, now
looking down
I see my own
beard, i.e., without
a mirror. This
has never happened
before. What
more could a man
desire? What more?

### TWENTY-THREE

Does my old apple tree in
bloom have a million petals,
William? The magnitudes
always defeat me. But what
abundance! What plenitude!

## TWENTY-FOUR

Do you know, William, that the male testes
produce 70,000 sperm cells a minute? When
you nap for an hour you create a city
the size of New Orleans or Cleveland.

## TWENTY-FIVE

What is the Now,
William? To my mind
it is Essential Ignorance,
in which we exist
forever. But can we
rejoice in it?
Should we?

## TWENTY-SIX

The ladybug swarms
in the red autumn,
William. She
and her many sisters
seek something at my
door. A place to lay
the minute hopes

of the next generation
or a place to sleep
for the winter? I'm
not sure. I thought
I'd open and let her
in. And my wife said
I could if I wanted.

## TWENTY-SEVEN

Like a babe in the woods,
William – think what
it must have meant.
A small child strayed
from the compound
into the forest; frantic
cries of the parents, neighbors
running and running. And
out there the wolves,
the big cats, the hungry
bears, the great darkness.
Tenebrosity. And now
we use the phrase without
a moment's thought.

## TWENTY-EIGHT

Who in this old and worn-out world
can yet resist the melody of words,
William? I think before long we
will be the death of everyone,
you and I and Shakespeare and General Patton.


## TWENTY-NINE

In dividing a pie, William,
some people prefer
eighths and some people
sixths. But Mary Oliver and I
think quarters are right.


## THIRTY

The frightened and lonely
        old man, William,
who has one glass too many
        is very likely
to find himself dialing
        800-numbers
randomly at two o'clock

in the morning
just to find someone
to talk to.

If you know a composer
more boring, William,
than Gustav Holst, call up
the NPR and they'll
be glad to play the music
of your recommended
annoyance every day.
Every blessèd day.

Barry asks if I prefer
to eat my apple pie
with ice cream or,
in the New Englander
fashion, with Cabot
cheddar. But William,
what can I say? I like
my apple pie all by
itself.

I must be some
kind of a purist after all.


THIRTY-THREE

It's been some time, William,
since I sent you a fax. Is this
thread of consciousness coming
to an end? See how the edges
of life fray and tangle like
the mane of an agèd horse.
Get out your currycomb,
William, and let the hairs
snag and pull as they may.
The pain is good for you.


THIRTY-FOUR

In the middle distance with the old white pine
in the background a monarch drifted down
almost like a falling leaf but slower
and more irregularly. This was at
the Dobynses' in New Hampshire, William.
What a peaceful place! – during the brief
hour when I was alone. Even the cooing
of the doves, insistent, demanding, offensive,
seemed for once more or less acceptable.

### THIRTY-FIVE

Who wants to live in a country,
William, that during one's
Whole lifetime has persistently
And internationally insisted
On the sanctification of avarice?

### THIRTY-SIX

All this absolutely irrelevant, insistent
Blather, William, about beauty –
And the nearly hairless human animal
Is the ugliest thing that ever evolved on this planet.

### THIRTY-SEVEN

Backlighting, William, is one
of the wonders. The way you
look through the trees of the woods,
through the limbs and ragged foliage,
through the confusion, toward
the little clearing ahead
where the sunlight is flooding in.

### THIRTY-EIGHT

In the rain, William, your voluptuous
peonies surrender entirely, laying
their tousled heads on the ground.


### THIRTY-NINE

William, I've come to a kind of a conclusion.
The old-time pentameter ain't that bad a beat.


### FORTY

William, the nicest thing about
clarinets is that they don't care
who plays them or what kind
of music is played on them. Would
that we could do as well, William!


### FORTY-ONE

The only way we can do anything, William,
is by understanding that every action
performed in this vain world, from buying
a pound of coffee to visiting a friend
in Peoria, is an act of mercy.

### FORTY-TWO

William, my wife is a fine and remarkable
person who has made the best home for me
I've ever had. And what's especially nice
is that she says the same thing about me.

### FORTY-THREE

Consider, William, this truly American
word, *gonna.* The President uses it,
and so, alas, does the Chief Justice
of the Supreme Court. And so,
double alas, do I. How could such
a disgusting locution have crept
into our habits of speech? William,
it's a very frightening sign.

### FORTY-FOUR

"Is faith not also natural?" So said
the woman yesterday in Utica.
William, why is it so hard
to convey a simple, obvious idea?
When human beings abandoned
the other animals, we left behind
the right to behave instinctually –

I've said it a thousand times. But she
looked at me as though I came from Mars
instead of Connecticut. Good grief!

"Form follows function," William.
How neat, how simple. And how like
Mother Ann in her Shakerish tact.
Self-evident too – for just look
At a chair or a wall. Perfect. But
Unfortunately Mother Ann some-
How failed to inform us of just what
The hell the function of a poem
IS!!!

Red tape and foolish effort,
William, are what this outrageous,
moribund, and postliterate
society demands from its elders,
while what we should be giving
is our wisdom. I am dead
serious about this, William,
and not a little angry.

### FORTY-SEVEN

Inevitably someone, William,
will be glad when you're dead.

### FORTY-EIGHT

To repeat, William, inevitably
a whole lot of people will not
miss you once you are gone,
and those who do won't miss you
all that much. Talk about personal
bleakness, William! Christ, it's
enough to be the death of anyone.

### FORTY-NINE

You say I shouldn't write
so much about old age?
Well, William, I expect
that's true. But I always
told my students to write
about what they know, and
tell me, William, what
the hell else do I know now?

### FIFTY

I don't know about yours, William, but when
I warm up my morning muffin in my microwave
the digital timer counts down the seconds in-
exorably, flip, flip, flip, until, when my muffin
is ready, the word END pops up grinning
like a fox in the henhouse. Sometimes, William,
in fact rather often, we must marvel at the
metaphysical acumen of the technologists.

### FIFTY-ONE

The Brahms sonata for clarinet,
William. I remember practicing it
for hours and hours. Now when
I hear it performed by Reginald
Kell, I realize just what an annoying
pain-in-the-ass I must have been.

### FIFTY-TWO

*Nonce,* William, is a good word
meaning (in my etymology)
not once, i.e., never, i.e.,
my chance of winning the lottery.

Also meaning a word never
used before. Okay then. Here
goes. Sallu squatfrig! And let
the bad times roll. Amen.

### FIFTY-THREE

William, last night I was watching
the sports illustrated swimsuit program
on the degenerate tube, and I swear
if I saw one of those young women
running naked through the woods I'd
turn away in disgust and go looking
for a bobcat, a wood rat, or a pretty vixen.

### FIFTY-FOUR

Eight to the bar, William, as
Pete Johnson, the great one, said.
And then let's just boogie on out
of here. It's the way to go.

# PART V

# Bashō

# WHILE READING BASHŌ

### COMPARATIVE LITERARY ECONOMICS

Bashō, you made
      a living writing haiku?
            Wow! Way to go, man.

### IT'S TRUE

The night left flowers
      of snow in my plum tree. Now
           the wind is rising.

### NAMES IN THE WIND

Bashō, I like your
      real name. Matsuo. Mr.
           Matsuo to us.

It has a certain
      ring, no? Yes. My real name is
           Teddy Roosevelt.

The Buddha said – at least I think he did, but I'm
      never sure of these things –
            that the "self" has no independent

existence. Wouldn't it be better
      to say that existence has no independent
            existence? This twenty-year-old

beech tree in the woods on the hill is growing
      out of a snarl of rocks, its roots
            twisted and gnarled. I've never

seen anything like it. Well, of course. I've
      never seen anything like anything.
            If this isn't independence

then I'm from Mars. But is it
      existence? I'm never sure, but yes,
            I'm inclined to doubt it –

here on this scrabbly hill in the
      unrecognizable center of the predicament
            that many people call New York.

## SATURDAY MORNING IN MUNDANE MUNNSVILLE

It's true, ignorance was... well, not exactly
bliss, but at least a comfort. I didn't know
that a millennium of complicated literary
history, Chinese and Japanese, poetry, fiction,
and copious theory, came before Bashō.
For years I didn't have to study it.

## SATURDAY WAS THE FIRST DAY OF THE NEW MILLENNIUM

The risen sun seemed to him like an oyster
        behind the overcast, smiling there. A pale
bloom as remote as Siberia. And how the world
        converts its ordinariness to beauty, he thought,
as he lighted a cigarette and puffed the smoke
        against the window, curling like petals. Why
is it so hard to get rid of time? Now is always
        a moment, an infinitesimal fraction of a
moment, inapperceptible. Yet the oyster smiles
        and the millennium begins, whatever that is.
Already the millennium is beginning to disappear.
        A gray morning, and the windowpane is cold,
and beyond it the soiled old snow is tattering.
        Is it because so soon I am going to die?

## SHARING

The snow falls. Bashō,
     we are very far apart
          and snow is falling.

I'm almost eighty,
     and as I watch the meadow's
          brown grass vanishing

beneath this whiteness
     how can I not share with you
          the poignancy of

passing time?


## THE MATTER OF HUTS

After the setbacks
     of Chicago and New York,
          he went to Vermont,

to a cowshed nine
     feet square. Was he proud to
          learn that Chomei's hut

in the mountains near
            Kyoto had been "ten feet
                        square"? Maybe. Who knows?


### HISTORY

A long time ago,
            far back in the obscurest
                        recesses of time,

a *poète innom-*
            *mable* murmured his praise to
                        a twisted sapling

on a mountainside
            in Japan, and the scarcely
                        emergent human

spark of consciousness
            brightened like a gleaming leaf
                        in the forest. No

other occasion
            in all our lives has been as
                        important as this.

## SOCIOLOGY

Ron Martin says that
       where he lives men are men, and
          the sheep are nervous.


## INEXPRESSIBILITY

Neither this brilliant
       intricate flower on my
          hibiscus nor this

clump of words can say
       anything at all. Beauty
          and sadness guide me,

inexpressible.
       I water the hibiscus,
          and I play with words.


## TEA CEREMONY

I wonder, can you
       do it equally well with
          vodka martinis?

## THE GRAVE OF RYŌKAN

When my friend Sam went to the temple Ryusen-ji
      where the grave of Ryōkan is located
He was, he says, "unspeakably happy" and filled
      with an inner lightness,
Which disconcerts me. Have I ever in my life
      been unspeakably happy? I don't
Know what it means, certainly not if it
      means standing at a grave-site.
Old moldy bones down there. Sam, you are
      blessed. And I'm a sad-assed heathenish Yankee.


## GLASSES

Why do I polish
      my glasses? In middle age
            I rarely bothered,

just swiped the lenses
      with my shirttail. But now my
            eyes have looked too often

through the smirch of life,
      all the fingerprints. Now I
            need a vacant view.

## MEDITATION

*Zazen, rōhatsu —*
        fierce unfamiliar words that
                mean meditation.

Mean kneeling beneath
        the priest's thwacking stick to learn
                while the sutra thrums.

Once by a pool I
        knelt in the Waterville Notch
                to watch the pretty

salamanders float
        in their passionate claspings.
                I knelt for three hours.

## ARMCHAIR TRAVELER

Ah, how charming, how
        like a painting. I see red
                barns and white church spires

among the elms, there
        not far from Kokujo-ji —
                never-never land.

## EMPHYSEMA

Had you air, Bashō?
        I mean enough to climb those
                mountains? Or did you

stop every ten steps,
        leaning on your staff and gasping
           like a fish ashore?

## BAD DAYS

Another awful day. Pain everywhere.
        Exhaustion. My spleen and kidneys shaking
from the cold. And yet I was embraced by my
        stunningly beautiful woman and by this
long-dead Japanese wonder-poet. Indeed
        even on the bad days good things happen.

## A WONDER

How astonishing
        at ten-thirty when the fog
           burns off and reveals

The World!

Shogun Iyeyasu planted sixteen thousand cedars,
　　　the Japanese cryptomeria, surrounding
the shrines and temples in the mountains at Rin-no-ji, or
　　　rather he had hundreds of workers plant them while
His Smugness looked on in exemplary satisfaction.
　　　No doubt he walked among them, congratulating
himself on his sanctity. I write of this in Roman
　　　meters long descended and attenuated
because I myself have planted a white birch, a tulip
　　　poplar, two oaks, and four Juneberry trees on this
hill in North America, neither western nor eastern.
　　　I dug the holes, sifted the soil around the roots,
added compost, and in the long drought lugged water, gasping
　　　for breath, up the hill to pull my saplings through. I
rejoiced in their success and felt close to these new friends here
　　　in my isolation, just as I rejoiced in
the variousness of the world. But the shogun should have
　　　planted a tree himself if he would know the true
sanctity. At least I'll tell him this, though I have no
　　　shrine in North America, nor any need of one.

## ELEGANCE

No elegance is
       ascribed to sweat: dripping from
           the carpenter's nose

onto the clean ply-
       wood. Yet I recall in my
           big sheepskin how I

sweated in the snow,
       heaving the axe and peavey,
           and how sweet it was.

And how jubilee
       cried in jay-song to the gray
           sky, and the white owl

sailed on extended
       wings unerringly among
           the snow-clad spruces.


## ACTION

"Action is measured
       by inaction, inaction
           informs action." So.

I am enlightened.
Yet in my language I find
no word for action.

How can I translate
an act into a concept
when they both are dreams?

I'm an old man. Yet
I knew this when I was young,
when I was unborn.

### KANNON

In Japan, where I have never been, Kannon
is the name of the Buddha of Compassion, and many
temples have been built where worshipers gather,
beautiful temples of wood and stone, bamboo and paper,
with gardens all around and groves of flowering
trees. So I am told by many authors whom I
respect. Yet I am struck now by the thought that
temples of compassion exist all over the world,
wherever you find a house in which two people
have lived together for a long time in mutual
concern and loving-kindness, for each other
and for the world. One such temple is in the
Stockbridge Valley, on East Hill just off the Bear Path.

Often and often
      I thought of Ophelia drowned.
        Her image always

in the shallow stream
      invading my dreams and days,
        loveliness in death.

But now I know: she
      is hideous. Her features
        are melting, the bone

of her face shows through,
      her hair no longer blonde but
        muddy and matted,

her garments awry,
      revealing a sunken breast
        with its green nipple,

and her pretty feet
      twisted sideways – they will not
        ever walk again.

The stream, unheeding,
      flows on, the implacable
        and timeless water.

And now the clangor,
      how it inflates the wind with
          ambient madness,

for surely we are
      there. Attending our betrayed
          sister forever.

### THE CARVED STONE

Where Bashō had tea
      his famous "summer grasses"
          swish now in the wind.

### SUMMER AFTERNOON

Buddha triumphans.
      Meditating trees. Even
          the goldfish are still.

# PART VI

# Second
# Scrapbook

# THE FANTASTIC NAMES OF JAZZ

Zoot Sims, Joshua Redman,
Billie Holiday, Pete Fountain,
Fate Marable, Ivie Anderson,
Meade Lux Lewis, Mezz Mezzrow,
Manzie Johnson, Marcus Roberts,
Omer Simeon, Miff Mole, Sister
Rosetta Tharpe, Freddie Slack,
Thelonious Monk, Charlie Teagarden,
Max Roach, Paul Celestin, Muggsy
Spanier, Boomie Richman, Panama
Francis, Abdullah Ibrahim, Piano
Red, Champion Jack Dupree,
Cow Cow Davenport, Shirley Horn,
Cedar Walton, Sweets Edison,
Jaki Byard, John Heard, Joy Harjo,
Pinetop Smith, Tricky Sam
Nanton, Major Holley, Stuff Smith,
Bix Beiderbecke, Bunny Berigan,
Mr. Cleanhead Vinson, Ruby Braff,
Cootie Williams, Cab Calloway,
Lockjaw Davis, Chippie Hill,
And of course Jelly Roll Morton.

# BIG JIM

The only man I ever knew who put
vinegar in his whiskey was Big Jim
Cannizzaro that worked down to the
quarry where he was in charge of blasting.
When he built his house he covered the
interior walls with the tops and sides
of old DuPont dynamite boxes with the labels
showing. "Reminds me of my place
in the world," he said, which is probably
also why he put vinegar in his whiskey.
"Hell, you put it on cabbage don'tcha?
Whiskey is the poor man's cabbage." Who
could dispute him, especially since he was
six-foot-three and weighed two forty-five?
He could hoist an eighth of a ton of
limestone onto his shoulder like it was
a bushel of chaff. But he never hurt
nobody. He had a big stone-colored cat
named Agri, and every night the two
slept together on his cot, both of them
well-oiled on vinegar and whiskey.
And he kept a full box of dynamite
under the sagging springs, just in case.

# END OF WINTER

### 1

Winter ending in the last days of March. How many times
        has the season
come and gone, with this soft inexorability? Bare patches
        in the meadow,
snowmelt tricking down the hill in hundreds of little
        channels, steam rising
from the sugarhouse across the valley. Someone is busy
        over there.

### 2

A redwing is singing in the willow tree, such a cheerful
        song. *Ocheree,*
*ocheree.* When he flies, his crimson shoulder-patches flash
        in the air,
not a spark, not a gleam, not an intimation, but a redwing
        flying.

### 3

What is the quality of life exactly? The remnant of ego has
        extinguished,
like the cone of ash in the beautiful Hindu incense-holder.
        It is not dying,

but dead. Sensation is what remains, the deep twinge of
                    pain with every
movement, or without movement. And then the softness
                    and warmth
of lying together, body to body pressing, such a comfort,
                    such a power
in the exchange of indefinable and sourceless and
                    incessant affection.


4

Don't use so many adjectives, said the man of fame. But
                    after all, now,
in the season of ending, what's wrong with adjectives?
                    They are only words.


5

Nothing green. But the willows are yellow, and so are
                    the beaks
of the starlings. Some new scent must be rising from
                    the ground,
the dog runs in the meadow with her nose down,
                    scattering snow,
leaving big wet paw-prints in an unintelligible pattern, like
                    the stars.

## 6

The house also changes, a little. Light is bright in the
windows. The dust
of winter appears, smoke clinging to spiderwebs, old
newspapers and letters.
Pain lies on the table like a handful of foreign coins. The
cat is yawning.


## 7

Water gurgles when it runs. Birds sing when they are
moved by hunger.

# HER SONG

She sings the blues in a voice that is partly
Irish. But "music is international." Singing
With her blue eyes open, her auburn hair
Flung back, yes, searching a distant horizon
For a sometime beacon or the first glimmer
Of sunrise. She sings in the dark. Only her own light
Illuminates her, although in the shadows
Are dim shapes, motionless, known to be
The tormented – in the bogs of Ireland, in
The bayous of Louisiana, relics of thousands
Upon thousands who suffered unimaginably
In ancient times. And in her husky contralto
They are suffering still. Knowingly she sings.
Music is anthropological. This is a burden,
For in her song no one can be redeemed.

# LETTER TO DENISE

Remember when you put on that wig
From the grab bag and then looked at yourself
In the mirror and laughed, and we laughed together?
It was a transformation, glamorous flowing tresses.
Who knows if you might not have liked to wear
That wig permanently, but of course you
Wouldn't. Remember when you told me how
You meditated, looking at a stone until
You knew the soul of the stone? Inwardly I
Scoffed, being the backwoods pragmatic Yankee
That I was, yet I knew what you meant. I
Called it love. No magic was needed. And we
Loved each other too, not in the way of
Romance but in the way of two poets loving
A stone, and the world that the stone signified.
Remember when we had that argument over
*Pee* and *piss* in your poem about the bear?
"Bears don't pee, they piss," I said. But you were
Adamant. "My bears pee." And that was that.
Then you moved away, across the continent,
And sometimes for a year I didn't see you.
We phoned and wrote, we kept in touch. And then
You moved again, much farther away, I don't

Know where. No word from you now at all. But
I am faithful, my dear Denise. And I still
Love the stone, and, yes, I know its soul.

# LITERARY NOTE

I remember a time in our moderate clime
    When the anapest ruled supreme,
And a great many folk who would babble in rhyme
    Used it until you could scream.

# MEMORY

A woman I used to know well died
        A week ago. Not to be mysterious:
She and I were married. I'm told
        She fell down dead on a street in
Lower Manhattan, and I suppose
        She suffered a stroke or a heart attack.
The last time I saw her was in the spring
        Of 1955, meaning forty-four
Years ago, and now when I try
        To imagine her death I see in my
Mind a good-looking, twenty-nine-
        Year-old woman sprawled on the pavement.
It does no good to go and examine
        My own ravaged face in the bathroom
Mirror; I cannot transpose my ravage-
        Ment to her. She is fixed in my mind
As she was. Brown hair, brown eyes,
        Slender and sexy, coming home
From her job as an editor in a huge
        Building in midtown. Forty-four
Years is longer than I thought. My dear,
        How could you have let this happen to you?

# MY DEAR ODYSSEUS

Well, I too have found my Nausicaa. When
I was sprawled in pain on the rocks, I looked up,
And there she was – in the mid-distance, composed
On the sand and brushing her long auburn tresses.
And what we have done on the way to her
Father's palace, which we have yet to reach
(For she leads circuitously through the woods and fields),
Is probably best left to your resources, dear
Odysseus, to your knowing and generous imagination.

## NO-MEN-CLA-TURE

When our friend Tony from Brooklyn was visiting
He glanced out the kitchen window at the bird-
Feeder and said, "Ah, look at the yellow chickadee!"

And why not? We've been calling them yellow
Chickadees ever since. After all, a name is
Determined by its object, or at least it should be.

But you go on calling them goldfinches if you want.

# THE PHYSICS AND METAPHYSICS
## OF THE PARTIAL PLATE

Who said I have to carry this mousetrap
in my mouth? Goddamnit, WHO? That
son-of-a-bitch judge had no right to
hand down such a sentence. It's *wrong.*
The whole freaking system is corrupt.

# SENILITY

To experience senility, to become
Senile, watching, day after day,
Week after week, the mist gathering
Around me in this little valley,
Descending from the hillsides, creeping
Along the creek-bed, grayer and grayer,
Darker and darker, until I can hardly
See my name before my face... Well
Then, what else can anyone say?

## SOMETHING FOR THE TRADE

Please note well, all you writers, editors, directors
out there: when a phone call is terminated
by the other person you do not, NOT, hear
a dial tone. You hear a faint click and then
silence, absolute silence. The dial tone
cannot be heard until you yourself hang up
and then lift the receiver again. Further
note this: you cannot tell from the click
if the other person has hung up reluctantly
or desperately, softly or violently. It is only
the sound of a disconnected circuit. I've read
this error in a thousand books, I've seen it
in a thousand movies, and how so many
of you can be so unobservant, you who
call yourselves artists, is beyond me.

# SOMEWHERE

Somewhere in a craterlike formation
Of scalloped granite the snow falls all the time,
Even when the sun is shining, and were it not
For an alarming run of bad luck human
Civilization would have started there.

# THE CRUEL

What in this world can equal for cruelty
reactionary ignorance? The question popped
into my mind while I was driving to Morrisville
and topped the rise onto the flat fields where
snow drifts across the road, and sure enough,
my rear wheels slipped sideways a little. Yet
I thought nothing of it because the question
engrossed my mind. This was the day when the victims
of Attica, murdered by Nelson Rockefeller in the year
1971, finally won their case in the courts. Victims,
i.e., dead in the ground. Their descendants rejoiced.

# THE NEW QUARRY

The new quarry in Sheffield has driven my
friends there practically out of their minds.
The noise, the dirt! – my God, in their very
sanctuary where for years they had practiced
their insanities undisturbed. Well, the master
of Zen says, Detach, detach from your possessions!
Especially this little cranny of the planet that you
cherish. Ah, could I tell you, Galway, stories
of the people from Mars who've destroyed the woodland
next to me! Close encounters of the very unpleasant
kind. So let the quarry dust drift down on
your green fields and wonderful fireweed flowers,
just as the ash from Mount Saint Helens whitened
my friend, the lop-eared dachshund of Montana,
making him look more than ever like a
semaphore. The gods in their condominium
up there, Argus and Angus, Mankato and One-Eyed Jack,
are grinning. Let the sons of bitches grin.

# THEN

How fresh it was then, the world then, a sheet of
Clean white paper written with mountains,
The lake, pines, red-winged blackbirds raucous
In the cattails, a naked girl, the world then,
Itself, itself, without and before the evil
Of faith, always this has been my fantasy,
Behind every sight of filth, sight of myself,
Even in the wretchedness of displacement
Forever, this I have seen always, seen
In a firm and resplendent knowledge of what
Exists, unreachable behind my words and dreams.

# TIME, PLACE, AND PARENTHOOD

Here we are, my son, aliens in this place
That seems so remote from our origin among
The superb slopes and deep valleys of the Green
Mountains, only a day's drive to the east.
Most people nowadays think aliens
Must come from Mars, and indeed sometimes
I feel remarkably Martian, so apparent
Are even the little distinctions of time and place
To me in my old age. And sometimes also
You now in your maturity of body and mind,
Your handsome strength, seem so distinct from
The four-year-old boy who rode beside me
In our pickup over the mountains, or the six-
Year-old who built the hut under the roots
Of the half-washed-out hemlock by the brook,
That I can recall you only as in a faded
Photograph from another country. But no,
It isn't true, not for more than an instant. I still
Remember you clinging in my arms as we ran
Down the tilt of Marshall's pasture, or holding
My hand as we entered the little post office
In our old town, so loving, so loyal. In these,
My son, you have been constant; almost four

Decades later you are the same. My son –
My Bo, my David – my man now in this world –
Accept these words that can never say enough.

## TO A FRIEND WHO IS INCOMMUNICADO

What does it mean when a dear friend abandons
        her home, retires to a strange place of silence,
changes her phone to an unlisted number and
        remains dumb to every loving-kindness?
I have thought and thought, pursuing the spiral
        of conjecture through all the twists and turns
I know after a lifetime of suffering. Clearly
        catastrophe has entered her life. And now
the thought at the utter downmost end of the
        spiral is the worst thrust of human fiction
                imaginable. The gods truly hate us.

## TO MY YOUNGER FRIENDS

Let me remind you dear people
        that this is a poor man's house,
five rooms and jerry-built, hung
        on the bank by the highway, up
at one corner and down at another,
        with a tin roof, windows off-kilter,
containing between six and seven
        thousand books. One more, my dears,
will send it all tumbling onto
        the asphalt for the next eighteen-
wheeler to plow into headmost,
        for the greater glory of literature.

# TURNING BACK THE CLOCKS

The old man had played twenty-one losing
      games of computer solitaire and he
        sighed, acknowledging

the constant twins, Defeat and Bad Luck, Castor
      and Pollux. He stretched his arms
        upward and then

immediately, abruptly doubled
      over in pain from the cramp
        like Hamlet's rapier

through the arras into his back, and a small
      rumbling moan rose from him
        like a bubble rising

from a farting frog. The end of October. Bare trees
      and snow coming, winter coming,
        snow and silence in his brain.

Time to turn back the clocks,
      he thought. First the computer,
        which was simple, and then

the clocks on the microwave
        and coffeemaker, and finally
                his watch, turning the hour hand

forward around the dial for eleven
        hours as he had been taught to do
                almost eight decades ago.

Shuffling in worn-out slippers, he went
        to the other room and the clock
                there. This is the only ritual left

to us in which all people, rich or poor,
        young or old, still participate equally, he
                thought. So simple.

The rich cannot control it. The powerful
        cannot exploit it. Nor
                can those in poverty be

envious. Slowly he climbed the stairs,
        easing his shoulder along the wall
                to keep from falling,

falling into awful calamity. He reset
        his bedside clock and crawled
                beneath the jumble of covers.

He listened to the little song sung by
the October wind in the eaves
above his head. I should be

content, he thought. And for a
moment before he slept
he thought he was.

## ABOUT THE AUTHOR

Hayden Carruth, a longtime resident of Vermont, now lives in upstate New York, where he taught for many years in the Graduate Creative Writing Program at Syracuse University. He has published twenty-three books of poetry, a novel, four books of criticism, and two anthologies. Carruth won the 1996 National Book Award for *Scrambled Eggs & Whiskey,* and his *Collected Shorter Poems: 1946–1991* received the 1992 National Book Critics Circle Award. He has been the editor of *Poetry,* poetry editor of *Harper's,* and for twenty-five years an advisory editor of *The Hudson Review.* The Bollingen, Guggenheim, and Lannan Foundations, as well as the National Endowment for the Arts, have awarded fellowships to Carruth, and he has been presented with the Lenore Marshall / *The Nation* Award, the Paterson Poetry Prize, the Vermont Governor's Medal, the Carl Sandburg Award, the Whiting Award, and the Ruth Lilly Prize.

The Chinese character for poetry is made up of two parts: "word" and "temple." It also serves as pressmark for Copper Canyon Press.

Founded in 1972, Copper Canyon Press remains dedicated to publishing poetry exclusively, from Nobel laureates to new and emerging authors. The Press thrives with the generous patronage of readers, writers, booksellers, librarians, teachers, students, and funders – everyone who shares the conviction that poetry invigorates the language and sharpens our appreciation of the world.

PUBLISHERS' CIRCLE

The Allen Foundation for the Arts
Lannan Foundation
National Endowment for the Arts

EDITORS' CIRCLE

The Breneman Jaech Foundation
Cynthia Hartwig and Tom Booster
Emily Warn and Daj Oberg
Washington State Arts Commission

*For information and catalogs:*

COPPER CANYON PRESS
Post Office Box 271
Port Townsend, Washington 98368
360/385-4925
www.coppercanyonpress.org

This book is set in ITC Bodoni™ Twelve Book
with heads set in ITC Bodoni™ Seventy-two
Book, designed by Sumner Stone, Jim
Parkinson, Holly Goldsmith, and Janice
Fishman in 1994 after research
into Bodoni's original steel punches.
Book design by Valerie Brewster,
Scribe Typography. Printed on
archival-quality Glatfelter Author's Text
at McNaughton & Gunn, Inc.